SRA

OPEN COURT READING

The Horn

SRA

A Division of The McGraw·Hill Companies

Columbus, Ohio

www.sra4kids.com

SRA/McGraw-Hill

*A Division of The **McGraw·Hill** Companies*

Send all inquiries to:
SRA/McGraw-Hill
8787 Orion Place
Columbus, OH 43240-4027

ISBN 0-07-569452-2
   3 4 5 6 7 8 9 DBH 05 04 03 02

Mort is big.
His truck is big.
Its horn is big.

If Mort pulls a cord, the horn will blast.

Mort pulls a cord.
It is torn.
The horn cannot blast.

Mort has a plan.

Mort pulls a cord.
The horn cannot stop.
It is stuck.

Mort acts fast.
Mort grabs a corncob.
He puts the corn in the horn.